THE 12 BIGGEST BREAKTHROUGHS IN
ROBOT TECHNOLOGY

by Marne Ventura

12 STORY LIBRARY

www.12StoryLibrary.com

12-Story Library is an imprint of Peterson Publishing Company and Press Room Editions.

Produced for 12-Story Library by Red Line Editorial

Photographs ©: catwalker/Shutterstock Images, cover, 1, 17, 28; Bettmann/Corbis, 5; Marko Drobnjakovic/AP Images, 6; Bain News Service/Library of Congress, 7; Geoff Caddick/PA Wire/AP Images, 9; Bibiphoto/Shutterstock Images, 10, 29; Baloncici/Shutterstock Images, 11; SRI International, 13; NASA, 14, 15, 19; Denis Klimov/Shutterstock Images, 16; NASA TV/AP Images, 18; Keith Srakocic/AP Images, 21; Homestudio/Shutterstock Images, 22; ilterriorm/Shutterstock Images, 23; Jirsak/Shutterstock Images, 24; Naotake/Thinkstock, 25; Damian Dovarganes/AP Images, 26; Google/AP Images, 27

ISBN
978-1-63235-016-9 (hardcover)
978-1-63235-076-3 (paperback)
978-1-62143-057-5 (hosted ebook)

DISCARD

Library of Congress Control Number: 2014937352

Printed in the United States of America
Mankato, MN
June, 2014

12 STORY LIBRARY

Go beyond the book. Get free, up-to-date content on this topic at 12StoryLibrary.com.

TABLE OF CONTENTS

1

AUTOMATONS PROVIDE INSPIRATION FOR FUTURE ROBOTS

In 1768, Swiss watchmaker Pierre Jaquet-Droz introduced The Writer. It was like a wooden doll but with mechanical parts that moved on their own. The 28-inch (0.7-m) figure was carved from wood. Approximately 4,000 cams, gears, and rods turned inside. It sat at a table and wrote up to three lines of text. The Writer dipped a quill into a pot of ink. Its eyes and head followed its hands as they moved. Its motions made it appear lifelike. A wheel could be changed to make it write different words.

Automatons such as The Writer were an early kind of robot. An automaton is a machine that can move by itself in a repetitive manner. The Writer could be programmed to write different text. This set it apart from other automatons of the time.

Jaquet-Droz made two others. The Musician could play five songs on an organ. The Draughtsman could be programmed to draw simple pictures, such as a dog or a man.

ROBOTS

A robot is a type of machine that carries out a complex set of tasks automatically. Early robots, called automatons, were purely mechanical. They had moving parts, similar to a clock. Later, robots were controlled by computers. Some robots are made to resemble people. Others are built for specific tasks.

40

The number of letters or symbols The Writer could be programmed to write at a time.

- Automatons became popular in the 1700s.
- First mechanical device that could be programmed.
- Created interest in robotics.

Kings and queens all over Europe invited Jaquet-Droz to demonstrate his creations. People were amazed to see what they did. As word spread, inventors were inspired to see what else automatons could do.

An automaton created by eighteenth-century Swiss watchmaker Pierre Jaquet-Droz has the ability to sketch pictures and write poems.

TESLA INTRODUCES RADIO REMOTE CONTROL

In 1898, scientist Nikola Tesla introduced a new invention to an audience at Madison Square Garden in New York City. He put a small boat in an indoor pond. The boat moved without anyone touching it. Audience members asked the boat questions. It appeared to answer by blinking its lights. At first, some people thought Tesla was controlling the boat with

Students view Tesla's radio-controlled boat at the Tesla Museum in Belgrade, Serbia.

4

Length in feet (1.2 m) of Tesla's robotic boat.

- Introduced by Nikola Tesla in 1898.
- World's first use of remote control.
- Called the birth of robotics.

Nikola Tesla was a Serbian-American inventor and engineer.

his mind. But he was using radio waves. He moved the levers on a small control box to send signals through the air.

Tesla was the first to use wireless radio control. His robotic boat was powered by batteries. Radio signals activated switches. The switches powered the propeller, rudders, and lights. Tesla thought the technology could be used to operate a variety of vehicles and machines from a distance. Tesla pictured machines fighting in wars instead of people.

But the US Navy was not interested in his technology. It was decades before Tesla's ideas were used. Because of his vision, however, he has been called the father of robotics.

THINK ABOUT IT

Many people were afraid of Tesla's remote-controlled boat. Why do you think they had this reaction?

CYBERNETIC TORTOISE DESIGNED TO LEARN

William Grey Walter was an English scientist who studied brain activity. In the 1940s, he started building small robots with simple artificial "brains." He used them to study animal behavior. His first two robots were shaped like tiny tricycles, with three wheels. He put a plastic shell over each tricycle. The pair of robots looked like turtles. He called them cybernetic tortoises.

The robot shells contained sensors, so the tortoises could tell when they bumped into something. They could also sense light. They used their sensors to move, the way that animals use their senses to find their way. The tortoises moved toward light. If they bumped into something, they backed away and took a new path. Later, Walter built a cybernetic tortoise that reacted to whistles to change its behavior.

Walter showed that by breaking down the way a brain works into steps, he could make a machine act like an animal or a human. These ideas laid the foundation for robots with the ability to learn and act in complex ways.

WHY ROBOTS?

In 1920, Czech playwright Karel Capek wrote a play called *Rossum's Universal Robots.* In the story, a company makes human-like machines to do work that people don't want to do. In the end, the machines rebel against the people. Capek chose the name "robot" from *roboti,* an old Czech word for slave labor. The name stuck.

An employee at London's Science Museum inspects a cybernetic tortoise invented by William Grey Walter.

8

Number of cybernetic tortoises built by William Grey Walter and his assistant in the 1940s and 1950s.

- Cybernetic tortoises were introduced in 1948 by William Grey Walter.
- Used light and touch sensors.
- Led to robots that can learn and behave in complex ways.

4

ROBOTIC ARMS JOIN ASSEMBLY LINES

In 1913, Henry Ford introduced assembly lines in his car factories. The process was divided into steps. Each worker performed one step, over and over. Goods could be produced more quickly and cheaply in this way. But workers grew tired of performing the same task. Some of the work was dangerous. Workers often had to use heavy, hot, or sharp materials.

Since the success of Unimate, robotic machines have become commonplace at factories.

500

Weight in pounds (227 kg) that Unimate could lift and handle.

- Unimate was invented by George Devol in 1954.
- First programmable robot arm.
- Introduced robots to assembly lines.

In 1961, another car company, General Motors, introduced a robot to its assembly line. Unimate lifted and stacked hot metal parts from die-casting machines. The robot arm weighed approximately 4,000 pounds (1,800 kg). A computer on a metal drum controlled it. Unimate could lift and move parts exactly as it was programmed. It was accurate to within 1/10,000th of an inch (0.003 mm).

A robotic arm is used for welding.

Soon more industries were using robotic arms in factories. Robotic arms could do work that was difficult, dangerous, or unpleasant for human workers. They could also do jobs more efficiently and accurately. By 1966, factories were using robotic arms for spray painting, welding, and many other jobs.

5

SHAKEY TAKES A STEP TOWARD ARTIFICIAL INTELLIGENCE

William Grey Walter's robotic tortoises introduced the idea of machines that could mimic the behavior of living things. From 1966 to 1972, scientists at the Stanford Research Institute built on the concept of artificial intelligence. Artificial intelligence is the ability of a machine to perform tasks in a similar way to humans. It can include the ability to learn from past experiences or to solve a problem creatively.

The scientists at Stanford built a six-foot (1.8-m) box on wheels. They called it Shakey, because it shook as it moved. Shakey was run by a computer. The robot had a built-in TV camera and sensors to pick up information from its surroundings.

Shakey was the first robot to be able to do a task without being given step-by-step instructions. A researcher might tell Shakey to move objects around a room. Then Shakey made a map of the room and a plan for how to achieve the goal. It could even correct its course if an obstacle got in the way.

2004
Year that Shakey was inducted into the Carnegie Mellon Robot Hall of Fame.

- Shakey was developed from 1966 to 1972 at the Stanford Research Institute.
- Could complete tasks without instructions.
- *Life* magazine called Shakey the "first electronic person."

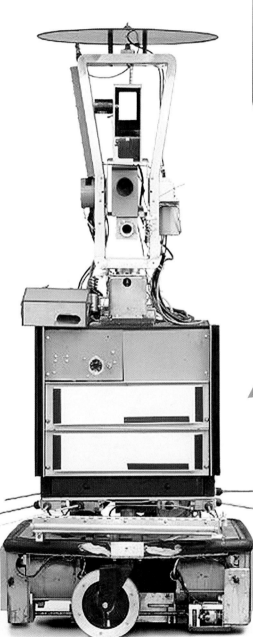

THINK ABOUT IT

Researchers have tried to make machines behave more like humans. What things do you think people can do that robots cannot?

Shakey is on display at the Computer History Museum in California.

ROBOTIC SPACECRAFT FURTHER SPACE EXPLORATION

A robotic spacecraft that carries scientific instruments is called a space probe. Without having to provide life support to astronauts, space probes are less expensive than manned missions. They also don't put any lives at risk. Space probes can visit places where humans wouldn't be able to survive with current technology.

Between 1966 and 1968, NASA sent seven robotic spacecraft to the

Viking 1 took this photo of the surface of Mars in 1976.

304

Days it took the Viking 1 lander to reach Mars.

- NASA introduced robotic spacecraft in the 1960s.
- Radio technology used to communicate with Earth.
- Lower cost, fewer risks than manned space missions.

COMMUNICATION

Before being able to launch a space probe, scientists had to figure out how to communicate with it. They learned how to transmit powerful electromagnetic waves in narrow beams through space. This allowed the spacecraft to send data it collected back to Earth.

moon. They collected information that helped scientists plan for landing a manned spacecraft there. In 1975, Viking 1 and Viking 2 were launched to explore Mars. They were the first spacecraft to land safely on another planet. The Viking landers looked for signs of life and sent back images and information on the planet's soil and weather. Since then, space probes have reached almost all the planets in the solar system.

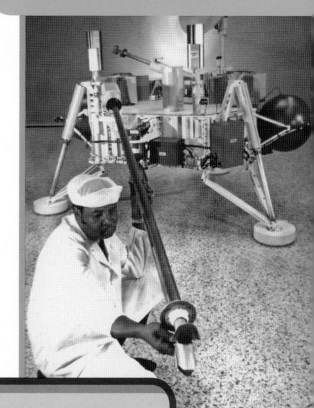

A NASA technician checks the soil sampler on Viking 1 before it is launched. The arm was designed to scoop the soil and deposit it in three scientific instruments for testing.

ASIMO ATTEMPTS HUMAN MOTION

Through the 1980s, many inventors had attempted to build robots that could behave like people. But no robot had been made that looked or moved like a person. Engineers at the Japanese car company Honda set out to change that in 1986. They wanted to design a robot that could walk on two legs like a person. It would be able to go up and down stairs and to walk on uneven ground.

The engineers worked for 14 years. They studied how human joints work and tried different techniques. Early robot models had only a pair of legs, with no upper body. The first one could take only one step every five seconds. The fifth model achieved a stable, steady pace. Sensors helped it keep its balance. Programs helped the robot adjust on uneven ground. Once the

Engineers worked for years to design ASIMO's legs so it could climb up stairs.

1.7

ASIMO's normal walking speed in miles per hour (2.7 km/h).

- Introduced in 1986 by Honda.
- First robot to walk upright on two legs.
- Designed to move like a human.

legs were working, the engineers added the rest of the body.

In 2000, Honda came out with ASIMO, a robot made to look and move like a human. Recent models can flip light switches, open doors, and sit down. ASIMO can recognize faces and sounds and answer simple questions.

BALANCE

The human body has several ways to keep its balance while walking. The inner ear senses speed and angles of movements. Muscles and skin give the brain information about muscle power, joints, and the ground surface. Engineers had to copy these functions to make a robot walk smoothly. They designed various sensors to give ASIMO the information it needed.

ASIMO is designed to mimic human behaviors, such as shaking hands.

RADIO-CONTROLLED ROVER EXPLORES MARS

NASA's Pathfinder reached Mars in 1997. A parachute dropped it onto the planet. Airbags opened to break the fall. A small robot called a rover unfolded. It rolled down a ramp and began to roam. Named Sojourner, the robot weighed 23 pounds (10.6 kg). It was approximately the size of a child's wagon. Sojourner held three cameras, tools to study soil and air, and solar panels for power. It was the first wheeled robot to explore another planet. It was also the first to be controlled by radio signals.

Earlier space probes had been controlled mostly by automated programs. Scientists were only in radio contact with the Viking landers for small portions of the day. But radio technology had improved by the time Sojourner was launched.

Sojourner rolls off the ramp after Pathfinder first lands on Mars in 1997.

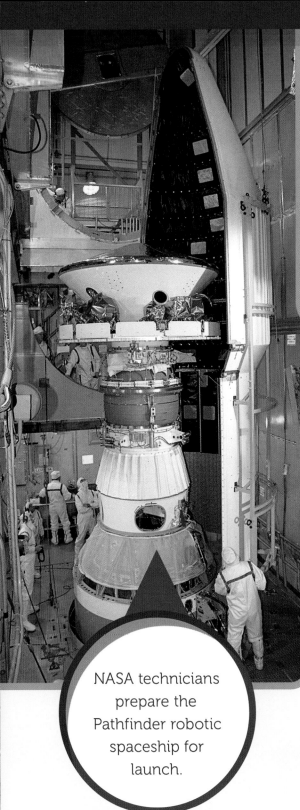

550

Number of images of Mars that Sojourner sent back to Earth.

- Introduced by NASA in 1997.
- First radio-guided spacecraft on Mars.
- Led to the use of smaller, lower-cost rovers.

Back on Earth, NASA employee Brian Cooper held the controls for Sojourner. It took more than 10 minutes for a radio signal to travel between Earth and Mars. Cooper would send a set of commands to the robot. Sojourner used its sensors to figure out the best route. It moved slowly, avoiding hazards. A while later, NASA would receive a set of pictures. Cooper could see if the robot had ended up where the scientists wanted it to go. Sojourner worked so well, soon NASA was sending more robotic rovers into space.

NASA technicians prepare the Pathfinder robotic spaceship for launch.

SOCIAL ROBOTS INTERACT WITH PEOPLE

Researchers at Carnegie Mellon University in Pennsylvania wanted to make a robot that behaved more like a person. They wanted it to be able to move around in public places and interact with people. In 1998, they introduced a robot named Minerva. Minerva acted as a tour guide at the Smithsonian National Museum of American History during a special exhibit.

Computers, sensors, and lasers helped Minerva get around. It could sense when a person was close. It rolled up to guests and interacted with them. It told them about the displays. Minerva could even react to the way people treated it. The robot smiled and sang when the tour group cooperated. It frowned and honked when people got in its way.

Minerva showed that robots could do jobs that involve interacting with people. The researchers used what they learned from Minerva to make two robots named Flo and Pearl. These "nursebots" were designed to live with an elderly person who was ill. They could help a person who needed assistance getting around. They could also provide reminders on when to take pills or call the doctor and provide social contact.

Another robot, Valerie, was designed to act as a receptionist. Valerie stood near the door to a building at Carnegie Mellon. It welcomed people, gave directions, and chatted about the weather.

THINK ABOUT IT

What jobs do you think robots should be designed to do?

500

Number of images Minerva took at the museum exhibit to make its own map for getting around.

- Introduced in 1998 by Carnegie Mellon University.
- First social robot.
- Able to interact with people.

Valerie, a "roboceptionist" at Carnegie Mellon University, greets visitors and answers the phone.

Roboceptionist

21

10

AIBO PUTS THE FUN IN ROBOTICS

Through the 1990s, most robot technology was being used to do work. But companies were starting to see robots in a different role—as fun toys. In 1999, Sony introduced a robot dog called AIBO, a Japanese word for "companion."

AIBO had two dozen motors inside. These moved its legs, tail, and head. It could do many things a real dog could do, such as scratch, roll over, play dead, or chase a ball. Its sensors and camera allowed it to see and hear. With its powerful microprocessor, AIBO could even learn. Over time, the robotic dog could grow to recognize its owner's voice and to understand some words and commands. AIBO could even remember where

furniture was placed in a room. To seem more like a real dog, it was programmed to express emotions, such as excitement or sadness.

AIBO paved the way for other lifelike robotic pets.

22

AIBO was one of the first robots available for consumers to buy for home use. Although it cost $2,500, the robot pet proved popular in its seven years of production. But Sony discontinued the dogs in 2006 when it overhauled all of its product lines.

150,000
Approximate number of AIBOs sold before Sony stopped making them.

- Introduced by Sony in 1999.
- Lifelike, able to learn over time.
- One of the first robots available for home use.

Sony's robotic dog could learn tricks or play ball, much like a live pet.

HOME ROBOTS MAKE CLEANING A SNAP

In 1990, a group of scientists from the Massachusetts Institute of Technology founded the company iRobot. At first iRobot focused on making robots to do jobs that were unsafe for people. They made unmanned machines called drones to search for landmines. They made robots designed to dismantle bombs. Then iRobot used similar

With robotic vacuums, people have more time and energy to spend on other activities.

technology to make robots to clean homes.

Roomba, the first home-cleaning robot, came out in 2002. The disc-shaped machine rolls around a room. Sensors inside help it map the area. Brushes under the disk spin and clean the floor. It senses dirty spots and works in those areas until they are clean. It rolls back to its dock to recharge when its battery gets low.

Roomba was one of the first robots small and inexpensive enough for home use. It proved that robots could be used for everyday tasks.

Since Roomba came out in 2002, many other companies have started to make home-cleaning robots.

10 million

Approximate number of home-cleaning robots iRobot has sold since 2002.

- Introduced by iRobot in 2002.
- First cleaning robot.
- Most popular robot for home use.

HOME ROBOTS

Since the success of Roomba, robots have been designed to do many household chores. Grillbot is a small, heat-resistant robot that can clean a grill. Robosnail is designed to keep aquariums clean. It moves around in the tank and wipes the slime off the walls. Other robots are designed to clean windows or mop floors.

ROBOTIC CARS COULD BE THE FUTURE

In 2005, the US Defense Advanced Research Project Agency (DARPA) held a contest. The challenge was to make a robotic car that could travel across 132 miles (212 km) of desert without the aid of a driver. Sebastian Thrun, a researcher at Stanford University,

decided to try. He and his team made Stanley, a self-driving car. It competed against three other robotic vehicles and won a $2 million award for Stanford.

Stanley began as a Volkswagen. Thrun added computers, cameras, global positioning system (GPS)

Stanford researcher Sebastian Thrun designed the self-driving car Stanley.

One of Google's self-driving cars navigates the streets of Mountain View, California.

technology, and sensors. Stanley mapped out the best path and avoided hazards. It made it safely to the finish line before the other vehicles. After the success of Stanley, Thrun teamed up with scientists at Google. They started to design self-driving cars that could work in cities. Driverless cars make fewer errors than humans. Some scientists think they could be safer options for the future.

Google employees have been test driving the cars in California. The cars always have a driver and a software engineer inside in case of an emergency. Based on the cars' performance, Google employees have been improving the software.

19.1

Stanley's average speed in miles per hour (30.7 km/h) during its trip across the desert.

- Stanley was built by Sebastian Thrun in 2005.
- First car to drive itself across the desert.
- Led the way for Google's self-driving vehicles.

FACT SHEET

- Robots can be designed for many purposes. Some do jobs that are difficult or unsafe for people. Some robots do tasks that people don't want to do, such as repetitive factory work or cleaning floors. Other robots have been designed to look, move, or behave like people.

- In 1495, artist and inventor Leonardo da Vinci drew designs for a robotic knight. The drawings showed ways for moving its arms, head, and jaw. These drawings are thought to be the first-ever design for a humanoid robot.

- Many ideas about robots have come from science fiction. In 1941, science-fiction writer Isaac Asimov wrote about the three laws of robotics in a short story. He wrote that robots can never hurt a human being, that they should always obey orders from humans, and that they should protect themselves.

- In 1977, the first Star Wars movie was released. The robot characters R2-D2 and C-3PO inspired researchers to develop new and better robots.

28

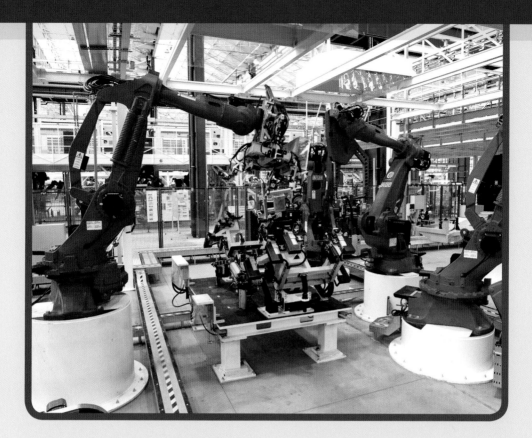

- Carnegie Mellon University established the Robot Hall of Fame in 2003. It recognizes important achievements in robotics technology.

- In 2002, researchers for DARPA began the Centibot project. The goal was to make robots work as a team. The Centibots built a map of a building. They worked together to find and bring back an object. Scientists hope one day Centibots will be able to work together to rescue people in danger.

- In 2012, the first humanoid robot, called R2, went into space. At the International Space Station, R2 does tasks too dangerous for human astronauts.

GLOSSARY

artificial
Not occurring in nature.

assembly line
An arrangement of workers and machines, each responsible for a step in the process of making a product.

automaton
A machine that moves by itself.

drone
A vehicle that operates without a driver inside.

electromagnetic
Using magnetism that is created by a current of electricity.

humanoid
Resembling a human.

intelligence
The ability to learn, process information, and respond to new situations.

machine
A manmade device with moving parts that moves or does work.

microprocessor
A device in a computer that manages information and controls what the computer does.

probe
A device used to collect and send information from space back to Earth.

program
Step-by-step directions for a computer or robot.

remote
From a distance.

sensor
A device that detects light, movement, or other information.

social
Interacting with humans.

FOR MORE INFORMATION

Books

Ceceri, Kathy. *Robotics: Discover the Science and Technology of the Future with 25 Projects*. White River Junction, VT: Nomad Press, 2012.

Kops, Deborah. *Exploring Space Robots*. Minneapolis, MN: Lerner, 2012.

Moss, Jenny. *How Robots Work*. North Mankato, MN: Capstone, 2013.

Stewart, Melissa. *Robots*. Des Moines, IA: National Geographic Children's Books, 2014.

Ventura, Marne. *Google Glass and Robotics Inventor Sebastian Thrun*. Minneapolis, MN: Lerner, 2014.

Websites

NASA: The Robotics Alliance Project
robotics.nasa.gov/students/students.php

Robot Hall of Fame
www.robothalloffame.org

Science for Kids: Robots
www.sciencekids.co.nz/robots.html

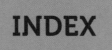

INDEX

About the Author

Marne Ventura is a children's book author and a former elementary school teacher. She holds a master's degree in education with an emphasis in reading and language development from the University of California.

READ MORE FROM 12-STORY LIBRARY

Every 12-Story Library book is available in many formats, including Amazon Kindle and Apple iBooks. For more information, visit your device's store or 12StoryLibrary.com.